Hamid Larbi

This Meadow of Words

poetry

Photographers

Maurizio Totaro
Samuel Duplaix

Translated by
Vatsala Radhakeesoon

Editions Dedicaces

First published by Editions Dedicaces in 2018

Copyright © Hamid Larbi, 2018

All rights reserved. No part of this publication may be reproduced, stored, or transmitted in any form or by any means, electronic, mechanical, photocopying, recording, scanning, or otherwise without written permission from the publisher. It is illegal to copy this book, post it to a website, or distribute it by any other means without permission.

ISBN: 978-1-77076-742-3

Hamid Larbi

This Meadow of Words

poetry

Preface

Is it a miracle, a deception, a weapon, a mask, the Quixote syndrome, a chemical hormonal dysfunction, a bleeding mountain or some madness?

What is it? Otherwise an act of love or hopelessness; may be a devilish possession or a state of deliverance or a disease? Who knows! However, I am sure it does not hurt; in fact sometimes it is beneficial up to the point of being therapeutic; it can become a universal cure for the wounds of the soul and whenever such a magical soothing effect is achieved, perhaps we are face to face with poetry.

I must admit that I'm not sure that I know what poetry really is. I had not felt such an emotional effect while reading Sapho, Dante, Rimbaud or Ginsberg as I did, in 1998, while participating in the gathering of "Mediterranean Poets for Peace" held in my land, Apulia. This was conducted in the presence of authors like Titos Patrikios, Mohamed Choukri, Jabbar Yassin, Nedzad Maksumic, Toni Maraini, Dijana Odeley, Izet Saraijlic, Giuseppe Goffredo, Angela Biancofiore.

It was during that gathering that I had established an artistic collaboration with Hamid Larbithat led us to poetry reading sessions together. We have been the chief -guest poets at various literary festivals.

Hamid took sheets of paper from his pockets like white pistols and began to read his poems by shooting words and lines about stars, revelations, flowers, tears, smiles anger and hugs like sugar-made and hemlock- made missiles about his(our) beloved Mediterranean region, whilst the audience and the moon maintained their tearful eyes and remained breathless.

"Hamid Larbi, asked one of the Literature professors who attended our poetry reading sessions at Laterza, a village in the gulf of Taranto, "Where can I buy your books?"

I intervened as I was from the neighborhood, stating that no book of Hamid Larbi had been published. "What a pity!" exclaimed the professor, "Not publishing such lovely poems is really a pity."

There are many people like that professor and I who ask that very question to Hamid; however, here we are, now fully-satisfied by his first poetry book "This Meadow of Words". I would surely look forward and appreciate the reviews of that book from professional poetry critics.

However, in my opinion, I confidently think that this book constitutes of all the major elements of outstanding poetry as it has been written by a rainbow-lover and reflective angel, my dear friend Hamid. Thus, I would strongly recommend it to all those hearts and souls who are still not engulfed by the mundanity of the business and technological worlds and still fly amidst the clouds and keep on dreaming.

NUNZIO TRIA
Writer

for my children: Iris and Elyan

The tongue defeated
It digs deep in the remains of forgotten memories
A vision sets up from the ashes
Speechless and refined

It is freed from fate
It flies beyond the essence
It dances at the rhythm of time
With an inexhaustible feeling
A path broken

By the destructive void
Invisible
without torment and colorless
That leads to degradation
By concealing the frightened tangible
And lost in the labyrinth

Engulfed by the endless fire of silence
It hints at me the spring breeze that blows
Lips warmed by the reflections of the sun
Irritated by the coldness of winter
It glues fragments of peace
It wins again the harmonious equilibrium
of the voice.

Figure 1 Copyright © Maurizio Totaro

Dark starless night
In silence, the abyss of a new risk
The snares entangle me
Much more tormented that the storm
The penance makes me feel ashamed
Hatred strengthens
Your vehement promises
Turn into disillusionment

A regret and a mere act of forgiveness
I have given you flowers and joy
Your gratitude is pain
A seed like a reward
The shame to observe me undergoing it

From my life only remains
Cold and dreary ashes
The zeal comes from the soul
And not from the impertinent reason
I desired you
But you were fated to belong to someone else
What am I waiting for?
A lenient, unstable part-time partner.

My day is a swollen pain,
That reveals only a single soft sound
But as night settles in, it floods
And I scream a verse all of a sudden
By expressing my call for my country
In order to meet an echo, a witness,
I share the heartfelt feelings
With my friends and unknown brothers residing far away
And my cry lingers, lingers, lingers
And when it touches the heart of my alter-ego,
Does he know that it comes from a painful night,
Without sleep and care ?
I can already imagine spring showering hope.

The reason, the body and the heart veiled
By those incomplete narrations
And those prohibited intoxications
As well as my fragmented dreams

Scattered by the wind
And buried by time
Only memories bear witnesses
Of those moving moments

Heaven engulfed by sorrow
In front of me, the sky closes and darkens
Those flames are immortal, I can't deny them
How much strength do I have? To live without a woman

No regret of using and abusing
Of that innocent stillness
The glance tracks beyond horizons
A magical flower remains
Deserted as the breeze blows.

Figure 2 Copyright © Maurizio Totaro

The solicitude takes shape on
Those trees undressed by the past season
With a hostile face
It hesitates about the path to choose
Dawn is all -grey
The moon eclipsed by the naked
Moments without scents
Without determination like sluggish leafy canopies
A cry without echoes and help
The desire for another season
That of generosity
And exaggerated love.

The enamored dream penetrates the mind
The body feels the urges of madness
Our desire is adorned like a rainbow
Our eyes get involved
in this madness all-excited
I cross each part of your body up till infinity
And I brush your body defying your shivers
Your heart languishes in the freshness
Beneath my passionate hands
An unconscious sigh
Produced by your tender lips
My present is in a trance
By savouring those moments
And the perfection of your gracefulness
It doesn't care about the duality
Between the old and the possibilities
I admire your sleepy figure
A glow of joy is displayed on your face
I would like to fall asleep and dream
Without feeling the need to ever wake up.

This mysterious star shines
When time is ephemeral
I meditate upon my deserted youth
To the persistent torture
Like the water flowing from a stream
Lost by the sea
Luck flees from my life
My humble and sincere passion
Devoted to selfishness
Of those who have loved me
has resulted in teaching me
that euphony is senseless
Amidst illusion and reason.
Pure pearls spring up
for those loves unfulfilled
giving me agony
The desert reveals in silence
The betrayal of time
I burn with the desire to light
The candle with the passionate one
Subtle verses are my only refuge.

Figure 3 Copyright © Samuel Duplaix

Tonight I discover the delights
by recognizing yours
A love that is more magical than the dream
Desire draws me to you
The desire to bring back to you
A tale of two lovers
Lovers without weariness
Lying on a flowerbed of signs
You surrender your body to me and I handle it carefully
The warmth of your desirable and moist skin
Leads me to the ecstasy of darwish
Your soft silky belly is so exquisite
I dare to caress this lovable skin
Hearing and enjoying
I have savored the sweet honey of your fountain
The perfume of your breasts diffuses in my veins
I already miss the excessive passion.

You have condemned me to this silence
Enclosed me within my throat
You have the art of doing and undoing
To build and destroy

You travel beyond the clouds
In quest of unknown fantasies
I have entrusted you my speechless past
I am a victim of the uncertain future

Now
I want to be held captive of my present
No one can retain me anymore
To lead my life in such chaos
By going towards an imaginary cosmic abode
And cover my world

Melting at the touch of the velvet
The mirage of creative writing
Encloses me in a coffin
It teaches me to walk on the ashes of the void

You are an incurable disease
Like my astrological sign
I veil my therapy
In this meadow of words
With some touch of Ivano Fossati's tunes
And another one from Pablo Neruda poems
Your closeness is soothing
These lexis don't make any sense
Without
Eloquence.

The emotional euphony of besame mucho
Finding the intimate shifting of desire
Going towards euphoric rhymes
Perfection is hidden in the shadow

Riding in the gloom
Spending nights burying
And un-burying those simple lives
The desert mocks at those whispers

Here comes the poetic emotions
A daily pittance
The soul flies fearlessly
Like the air, the sun
To describe one's conscience in words
That blows with metaphors
And take refuge in my mistress's climax of passion

A fountain of enjoyment
That is released from the interior warmth
Slides delicately towards you
Our bodies perfectly intertwined
Immersed with you and I
Breathe through your sigh
Please let's remain lovers.

Figure 4 Copyright © Samuel Duplaix

The shadow covered by dust
The land of swallows,
Dreams floating on the Adriatic,
Oh! Far away friends and without any news,
The face loses its glow,
The soul feels torn
Only a few memories
Of many past years
Of long and bright hours
Living vainly
More years left to meet death
Gradually
When you will be no more.

Figure 5 Copyright © Maurizio Totaro

An escape
Triggering strong emotions
Of auras sailing towards the infinity
Like my fate driven towards the unknown
Tunes created spontaneously on spot
Others already heard
Leading my senses into trance
Tuning the sounds of my fate
I follow my path at the will of my star
Notes fly and come back
Like the swallows.

The fresh breeze of the dunes
Still echoes
In this lost body
That requests me to have only virtue and desire
I give her my passion
And she makes a stop
Her glance is hostage and the delight of a trance
A rebirth of shudders
Time takes her away from my arms
With my soul quivering
I trace a circle of patience
In an endless tickled night
By the aphorism and her fragrance.

My mind is dried up
Unfortunately it is deprived of all sense of humour
Sterile
My sobs subside and I would like to forget them
Why have I been made to suffer?
Why is my heart destined to meet sorrows?
And unfulfilled loves,

I had won love and I had found my soulmate
And I was already believing in the immortal flame
As I am illogical
I didn't pay heed that that love was unconventional
I can't hold on such bitter tears
That flow down my face and are so precious to me

My heart suggested me lovely tales (fables)
And requested me to write on those flowers
Now, they are enclosed
In within this dark window
But it's useless
Poor child deaf and dumb
Who will try to understand your words?
And who will slide on your soul?
Time seizes me…
                …and it will kill me

I will remember your smile
As soft as blue dawn, exhilarating like a flower.

Figure 6 Copyright © Samuel Duplaix

The exquisite moments cheer up my memory
The cold wind blew on that fire
Once again my face expressing sad moods
And drenched by tears
Bitterness and melancholia predominate in my nature
The neutrality has emerged again

You mend and break my heart at your own will
Your silence is death-like
You suppress my breath that was filled with joy
The night transforms into an ocean
That drags me towards a wreck
The void transmutes my present
Bare of piety and virtue
And enclosing it in a catacomb

The joy of the lights flee
Turmoil jumps upon the remains
I had written verses by turning the pages of your feet
In turn I took only some spontaneous verses
Willing to escape this painful life
And rest all carefree
I do not spare you
There is no need to sympathize
To forget your possessive glance
My body still needs your closeness.

My imagination is consumed,
As the seasons go by,
By the passions for reason,
Devoid of my gracefulness and flexibility
I'm trapped in my ego
I drive into it and I'm carried to the depth
Of my distress
The weariness of eternity begins again
And from this great abandonment
The silent time tramples on the wounds
From those soft flashes of lightening
A piercing deception engulfs me
And digs the fatal void
For chasing tomorrow
Already stillborn.

Crawling from the top of the mountain
Amidst the shores
The song of the goldfinches
Coat of poppy seeds
Low walls illuminated with paleness
Suddenly I recognize that white chimney
In olive dresses
Surrounded by cherry-trees and fig-trees
The veils of lives
I wish to have a dawn completely filled with the sun
And no longer simply just for a moment.

Figure 7 Copyright © Maurizio Totaro

The torture to live without torture
The greed destroyed by reason
The past, an incurable wound
The fate internalized by agony
The mind vilified by secrets
And defeated by minuteness
Passion and bitterness are confounded
On a colorless cloth
The body rests
A ray of light
Ephemeral…
              … flies in the sky.

To wake up at night within you
To see again your smile
That is the source of all life
I imagine your lips
Smiling still in the dark
Kissing you passionately
and without laziness,
With soothing words and soft caresses
When I think about you
I can see you deep inside me
This desire emerging in silence
Warms me up by your accustomed body

To brighten with the light of your pleasure
By some vague caress
To be emerged in the cold waters of your lust,
Within you shifting, upon me screaming,
And those insane tribulations of the animalistic soul
With this passion that connects you and I
I would get hold of the sculptured lines
To create other words solely for you
To wake up once again upon your body

To brush your quivering and damp skin
That loves without insisting that it must be forever
I let my soul be exchanged in those kisses
You retrieve yourself in the freshness of the morning,
Without my noticing it
Leaving behind our desires intact.

The need for passion torments my horizon
I remember that life re-born
Each of your sweet kisses
Dispels in an unbounded beauty of its own

During the day, I follow the path that you trace
To fly a step ahead of your reflection
At night, I love you deeply
And I leave you at another passionate dawn

Far away, the dusk is blurred
Breathless due to the inability to reveal the dream
I melt by the neutrality
But I go on living

Believe me
We are drowning in the mud
By obeying the tune of resignation
The universe is just an illusion
I am not the guardian of your fate

You have been re-united with my emotional soul
A light of the joyful dawn
will replace your sufferings
If love is a riddle
Forgive me
If I didn't have time to learn it.

Figure 8 Copyright © Samuel Duplaix

The past shatters
Like drops of mercury
Fallen
The sky turns white
And you look at me from far behind
The speeches are lost amidst the branches
Bare of our souls
And time becomes
An enemy.

Figure 9 Copyright © Samuel Duplaix

I sail in a cradle on the waves of the sea
The sun kisses my face
The moon charms me by its eclipse
I have buried my face on a relaxing void,
And in the shadow of a bedsheet that plays with the wind
I open my mouth filled with ecstasy
I can no longer read what I've written.

The memory- nest engulfed by verbs
The blue flower bursts and reveals its grief :
Why can't I handle this fate
It's as if, it has been competing with time

I see your face again like a bright sun,
Your graceful hazel almond eyes urging reason
And your innocent glance diffusing like sea fragrance,
From your sublime mouth I have plucked your smile
Your heart rhymes with fulfilling naive words

With those surrounding trees, it's almost spring
Those places where our lovely space was founded,
In the closeness of our lips,
My senses and my soul still bear witness

Due to the call of your body, I stayed close to you the whole day
Which dream would have forsaken that dream in your Heart
Dream: hanging on a lighthouse
My caresses on your skin brings ticklishness
Your body and eyes are much more delighted than the facing sea

I can still hear your lips whispering "mia"[1]
My attention and thoughts pursue you
You are like the joy that can be easily described,
but like the soul of pleasure that is difficult to understand

The face of time didn't smile
I'm not alone, the governor of present
Be silent, O my heart. The morning will not give you that passionate kiss
Now regarding this love, it has always been forbidden
My only delight lies in having had loved you!
Everything ends in the shadow of a sign
Only illusion and songs
Still gently touch the walls of silence
And tears of intoxication well up without echo

---

[1] mine

Figure 10 Copyright © Maurizio Totaro

www.ingramcontent.com/pod-product-compliance
Lightning Source LLC
LaVergne TN
LVHW051712080426
835511LV00017B/2879